Alma Solitaria
By Ismael S. Rodriguez Jr.

A mind is like a parachute. It doesn't work if it is not open.
Frank Zappa

Table of Contents

Dedicated to my fellow Grey Witches

The Impermanence of Permanence

Listening to the wind
Blowing over empty space
For infinite seconds
Before time comes to a halt
Hold onto to nothing
And have nothing to lose
Existence for its own sake
Is glory beyond means
Harvest sweat dreams
From wishes of enlightenment
Strip away what isn't
Until all that's left is true
All things are permanent
Within their impermanence
Knock on Gods door
To find where it ends

Zen Noir

Living
Yes living
On the good side of dying
Darkness creeps in
And there's blood on the streets
Fight for survival little man
Everything's for the taking
If you don't get caught
Shadows within shadows
Try not to hold on to tight

Is It Time to Wake Up?

Drinking coffee smoking cigarettes
And watching porn
What a lovely way to start the day
The moon went down
And the sun came up
My habits seem strange
To the more normal crew
I like Suicide Girls
Especially a certain beautiful
Redhaired one
If I get enough money
I might pierce something strange
Or maybe a tattoo somewhere
I'd dye my hair too
If I had something
I could dye
But sadly, it seems
My forehead has
Gotten too big for that

Original Me

Particle dreams flash through my mind
Forgiving but still taking
Destroying facades of the ego
Until all that's left
Is the original me
Powers that be
Bring the fractured pieces
Of me back together again

Moon Spells

Within a circle of trees
Moonbeams caress you
While burning candles
Define these rites
The ancient mysteries
Are born anew this night
Scry the dark portal
The shadows abound
Where Hekate waits
Don't be ensnared
By the darkness within

Single Point

Pray they said and pray some more
But I don't pray to the same gods as you
I've got gods and goddesses
For different occasions
But they all dissolve back into one
Layers of reality contracting back
Into a single point
That is nowhere and everywhere

It's a Skill
(They Don't Teach in School)

Shit posting
Is a kind of poetry
That goes beyond
Your conceptions
Of what a poem is
Social medias finest
Displaying their skills
With much vigor
And running circles
Around the trolls

The Seven Deadly What?

It ain't a sin to be human
It's a gift that should be cherished
Do what thou will
That's all there is to it
We all have desires
Don't let them control you
But feel free to explore
Expand yourself in all ways
Mind, body, and spirit
Remember this truth
Life is to be experienced fully
On all levels of our existence

Set Yourself Free

Go ahead and testify
Then you'll purify
As you're flying higher
Powered by inner desire
Get to the next level
And deny your inner devil
Gnosis will set you free
And you can just be
Tear down every wall
When love comes to call
Children of the earth
Gia is the mother of all birth

Unity

Elder gods
Burrowing
Beneath your sanity
Bringing the unconscious
To consciousness
Reveal the dark
To enter the truth
Reveal the light
To enter unity

The Wrong Way Moon

I took a trip to Pickering's moon
It's an unusual place to say the least
With this going in reverse thing
But really, I'd have to say
It's a glorious diamond in the rough
It may not be a Janus as some may think
But its orbit is closer to my heart

My Hotdog

Look at my hotdog
It's like no other wiener
So tender and mild
It's a thing of beauty
A real work of art
If I must say so myself
Covered in pickle relish
My hearts one desire

Twenty-three and Five

What's a beginning
Without an end?
It's time to hail Eris
That's a way to start
Throw chaos to the wind
Take yourself out of neutral
If you're confused right now
Don't worry my friend
Everything is nonsense
If you believe what you read
Twenty-three and the five
If you look hard enough
Who knows what you'll find?
Take it out of the bun dude
At least that's what I've been told
The pathway to something
Is the one of least resistance
If you want it that way
If the goddess notices you
Maybe there's an apple
In it for you

Witness to Desire

Dancing angels sing
Spinning gods triumph
The never-ending dawn
Once dying embers flareup
Heaven's gate is shown
As daemons fly between
Eternity ends in a second
While the aeon lasts forever
The future is in the past
And the present never ends
Ten cities of creation
With twenty-two roads connecting
Rising to find the crown
That lies beyond the abys
Look behind the veil
The serpent now awakes

Wheelbarrow Full of Dreams

Visions flash through my mind
Like divinely inspired dreams
Bringing feelings of joy
And mischievous thoughts
It's the perfect end
To a brisk autumn night

Model Haiku

Goddess Diana
Goddess Diana
Most magnificent of all
Flowers in the dawn
Red Haired Maud
Maud is wonderful
The most beautiful redhead
Like no other woman
Italian dream
A blue haired goddess
A beauty like no other
Riae shines so brightly

Trip to the Moon

I went to the moon
Beyond the reach of man
To know all that happened
Is difficult to understand
My mind was playing tricks
That still confuse me now
Of, course it's my fault
A life coach said to me
The beauty of nature
Stunned my conscious self
Before I knew what happened
I suddenly began to rise
Flying through the atmosphere
And the space beyond
The man on the moon
Had the biggest smile
As I came closer to him
I came to a gentle landing
In the South Pole-Aitkin Basin
Then took a stroll around
Then rocketed back to earth.

Trip Through My Brain

I'm on a trip through my brain
As me cerebellum starts to drain
My pineal gland is decalcifying
To warm me of all the lying
It's my twenty-third time
To link to what is mine
My brain receives more information
On a corrupt and dying nation
The system failed us all
It's time to let it just fall

Divine Consciousness

Let's talk about life and dying
While having coffee and a smoke
They're both intimately connected
In this symphony we call existence
The universe is consciousness
And consciousness is god
Man is simply a reflection
Of that divine consciousness
We're working our way back
Into the mind of the creator
Make yourself a vessel
For the glory of the divine
And allow its light into your heart

Blue Haired Beauty

I have a thing for weird petite tattooed models
Especially when it comes to Italian blue haired ones
My thoughts center on her smile and her style is the best
Her body is a canvas off tattoos off artistic perfection
She's a true Mediterranean beauty like no other
And dances in my dreams like a goddess come to life

Time to Chill with a Kitty

There's this pretty kitty
That I'm proud to know
Who's really more than that
Her beautiful soul woke me up
To who I am now
And who I can make myself be
My love for her is endless
Her beauty runs deep
In mind, body, and soul
I won't call her one in a million
A woman like her is rarer than that
More like once in a lifetime
Or maybe once in a millennium

The Dark Carousel

The ride of a lifetime
Points to the shadows
Within our souls
Pagan ancestors bless
The challenges
Of the dark goddess
Free yourselves
By embracing all
Sides of our heart
Don't deny the darkness
Embrace it fully
Then transmute that power
Into healing yourself

Haiku

watermelons jump
colorblind horse mumbles, odd
deceptive disturbed
chambermaids' quake, broods
pull, amusing gory plump
sorcerer chases
querulous deathless
diamond cutter defecates
saxophone sobs, prim
earnestly blazing
swordsmen glower glumly star
ravages oozing
blossoming rainfall
braying chimera grins, stale
bemused mob sobs, sick
rugged ancient blind
plowman rejoices, massive shrill
green landlord squirming
Bela's follow, drops
emerge, gruesome giddy
raspberries drifting

BUSHKU

I just found out about these little beauties. Sorta like a Haiku but with 3-5-3 syllable count. Because haikus are too hard.

snakes dive... chiefs

whine... hard child fryin´

heads see... dumb

brave horse scores

oak spits... eel yelps... spoon

kills fiercely

soul runs... boat

cheers Tex-ly... great tan

star chokes... tame

wars score... hot

fish spoutin´ leanin´

cold pups grunt

doors call... rich

door peeks... gun cheers... drink

clucks... bag flops

heart falls... pig

leers... clear cat flees... mouse

trips - uh... blindly

Try to See

I got two eyes for looking
And one eye for seeing
The optics of spirituality
Is hidden from those
Who can't see the truth
One dimension up
And one dimension down
Forget about duality
The pendulum swings wildly
Back and forth continuously
All is in the one and the one is in all
Perform your absolutions
But don't be beholden to any god
Enlightenments within us all
Just remove what isn't

Gnosis of Self Answers always lead

To more and more questions
The more you learn
The less you really know
Look for the knowledge
Beyond the rational mind
With gnosis you understand
The real difference
Between ego and self
Remember you are the only
Guru that can enlighten you
Others may point the way
But you must walk it yourself
Trust your connection

With the divine
Over any teachings
Of religious leaders
Look to god to find yourself
Look into your heart to find god

Random Dark Sad Poems

One Last Hope Darkness descends
tortured
you once promised me an eternity
One last hope
Goodbye, my Love Don't pray for me
why don't you want me?
for the anguish eats away
your memories faded by time
Goodbye, my love
But I am still here
Goodbye, my love
Lisa We had a love so pure
always in a flash
forever in a minute
But our love was just a broken dream
you never believed
you never believed
we are now just two lonely souls.
The End of Days The shadow fades
a child,
a flash, a minute
bleak, torn
May wretchedness come upon us
When I Die you once promised me an eternity
gone with the wind
so it will be
a flash, a flash
When I die
I Miss You Now Take a bow
the hopelessness plagues

together as one always, you said
I am but a wilted flower
But I don't want to live
without a dream

Some Love Poems

The thrill of You I pray for your body,
joined together, I give you
joined together, I give you
You carry my kiss
you carry my soul.
For Diana, my love For Diana, my love
a candle, a stone, your body
a kiss in the ever life
like a golden sunrise
As I take an oath for always, my Diana
joined together, I bequeath to you
bound, joined, to never fall
You leave my soul
you share my pulse
Passion Beats As the passion beats into the future
bound, joined, to never loathe
your lips, a kiss through life
I melt in your passion.
My pledge As I pledge forever, my Maud
like a foggy shooting star
golden lips
Without your heart, shall invade
connected, bound, to never entangle
bound, bound, to never fall
I melt in your kiss.

Tequila shots in heaven When my days on earth are

done

and too the pearly gates I go

30

Eternal bliss will be mine
As I drink too God's creation
And all I've left behind
Know I'll love you always
And await our future reunion
As I have a drink for you
I'll walk the streets of gold
With those who came before
To be together once more
And have a drink with them

Soul Weary The state of the world

Makes my soul weary
Brother against brother
In a world full of hate
We are all an image of the divine
No matter the color of our skin
When did humanities love
Begin to fade away?
We're children of the same universe
Connected in spirit with all life
We need to love each other
And our wounded home
Be stewards of our beautiful planet
The earth cries out in pain
We must heal our mother
But we have to heal ourselves first

You're Disco Now God is a woman

And his name is Eris
Did you prepare
Yourself for that?
Your pineal gland

Connects you to him
And if you're reading this
You're a pope too
Everything you say
Is infallible, especially
If you contradict another pope

Fury Hellions Cats come from the devil's vagina

At least that's what they say
They're furry little hell spawns
That are fun to cuddle with
One kitty, two kitties
How about some more
The next thing you know
You're a crazy cat lady
We love the little beasts
All fur, tooth, and claw

Look at the goddess inside

Look into the depths of your soul
Tell me what do you see?
There's a goddess looking
Back at you my friend
Powerful and mysterious
Guiding you, teaching you
Exposing all that you are
To be critically examined

Headspace Burned out on logic

So, don't be a silly fool
Float in your headspace
My god your so cool
Dance with the devil
By the light of the moon
Philosophy is negated
So, I'll see you real soon
Mental abilities are gone
Who can think anymore?
It's so hard to focus
And my head is just sore

The Latino in Me I'm proud of my heritage

It goes straight back to Spain
With some New world blood
In my veins as well as
Some of the blood of Africa
My ancestors died for this land
The conquered and conqueror
Together inside of me

Make me stronger I think
I'm the descendant of
Proud brave warriors
And cultures so beautiful
They touch my soul

I Dream of Rain

I dream of rain
And the thunder roaring
Lightning flashing
Zeus unleashing
His furry on the world
The thunder god cleansing
All that is in his domain
Nourishing the earth

To Reach the All

Mystical practices mixed
With magickal rites
Polishing the mirror within
To reflect the divine light
The higher self
Reaches forever upwards
Seeking to fulfill
The ultimate goal
The kingdom is in you
A drop of consciousness
Containing all there is

Beautiful Dream

I had a beautiful dream
Just the other night
Man practiced love
And had no need to fight
We helped each other
Not because of some law
We knew the truth
It was good for all
All could do as they will
And humanity was free
No more hate or greed
A united planet of we

My Goddess

A goddess watches over me
I'm protected from harm
And guided on my path
Sometimes she's bathed in light
Other times she's in the shadows
Helping me to balance
The different sides of me
She's the source of all wisdom
And shows me what I need

Love and Tolerance

Spread your love around
Wherever you may be
Be a beacon of hope
For all the people of earth
As you grow in wisdom
Be willing to teach others
All that you know
Have compassion for all
Have tolerance for all things
Except for any intolerance

Awaken

The universe wants you to rise
To expand yourself
In every single way, you can
Awake to the enlightened
Divine master you are
Reach for the light
But don't deny the dark
Balance is the key
United and undivided

One Family

We are all one big family
No matter the color of our skin
Sons and daughters of the earth
Separated by false borders,
Ideologies, and philosophies
That we use to define ourselves
As different from others
And divide us from them
Let go of the hate in you
Embrace all as one

The Pendulum Swings

Duality doesn't exist
All things are one
Existing on a scale
As the pendulum
Swings back and forth
Sometimes to one side
Sometimes to the other side
Never resting in one place
Find balance within yourself
Don't let the swinging
Of the pendulum
Throw you off balance
Observe the movement
But stay in your center

Single Point

Pray they said and pray some more
But I don't pray to the same gods as you
I've got gods and goddesses
For different occasions
But they all dissolve back into one
Layers of reality contracting back
Into a single point
That is nowhere and everywhere

The Shadow and the Light

There are brief moments
Of unusual lucidity
When my subconscious
Starts talking to me
It's beyond my ability
To describe it to you
Words wont suffice
But it's in all that I do
I walk a difficult path
Balancing between both
The shadow and the light
Bringing about my growth

The Way

Live the life
Of love and light
In your deeds and words
Show others the way
Be understanding of those
Who have not traveled
As far as you have
Remember that you too
Were once in their place
Help guide people
As best that you can
Listen to the elders
But trust you're intuition

Eternity

Nothing is just eternity
Hiding from itself
Balancing on a point
That is everywhere
Within a circumference
That doesn't exist

Global Village

Love has sadly become
An extremely rare commodity
That's hardly seen anymore
I think that it's an oddity
What have we become
And is this the worlds fate
Loyalty only to our own tribe
But any outsiders we hate
Break out of the darkness
That the world has become
We are all stars trying to shine
Each and every man and woman
Forget about the old tribes
Forever fighting each other
We're a global village now
We are one big human family

The Cycle of Everything

Don't let your energy stagnate
Let it flow through you
Ever renewing and changing
Spiral cycles of life and death
Universal divinity mirrors
The divine in your heart
With angels whispering secrets
That your soul already knows
Grounded in mother earth
And rising towards the heavens
Connected with all eternity
Within the infinite now

Flow

Just flow with the Tao
And don't try to rationalize it
What you can rationalize
Isn't the true way of Tao
Tao goes beyond all explanations
And notions of duality
Opposites collide with each other
Canceling each other out

Points of Being

Unreal images rising
Through the mist
Marking delusions
That must be overcome
For the lower ego self
To be aligned with
The will of the divine soul
Knowledge and conversation
Your Secret Lover speaks
Listen carefully to everything
As you rise up the tree
Walk the pathways
Between points of being

Dance Dance

Existence is suffering
But there are tacos
Extra chilies for me
Forgot about tomorrow
I'll smile my blues away
Then put on my happy pants
And then dance a while
To the music in my head

La Petite Mort

Souls unite and egos diminish
As the point of ecstasy nears
The sacred union of goddess and god
Expressed in an act of human love
Lingam and yoni joined together
Fertilizing our very souls
With the universal energy
Of our divine progenitors' passion

Exclusive Party

While you were distracted
They purchased the country
And have the media tell you
What you're supposed to believe
It's a very exclusive party
And none of us are invited
Unless it's to participate
In one of their endless wars
Nothing ever trickled down
It was just more for the elite

Misery

Sometimes I can feel the depression
Creeping up in my mind
It's a feeling I know too well
And my opinion of myself
Gets worse by the minute
It gets harder to do anything at all
I just wallow in my misery
As the darkness cuts crushes me

The Japanese Within

At his seat, a fellow villager is bumming a smoke from a joint, and Kuroyuri is smiling mischievously at her. the person ahead of him, an older bearded Japanese gentleman, who's sitting within the back of the temple, hesitates, watching the 2 people with interest. the Japanese Priest leans back in his seat so he can recline against the wall—to avoid the pampering that Kuroyuri guarantees his worries, too. The young whiskered man bobs his head in an effort to seem denser, eyes magical, slipped in checked through a white sash bearing the kanji for dead. As Internal jokes go, this one doesn't accompany a bible. The 'Wisdom Within' (WIC) pick of the 'JAs' that apparently no one's giving him the maximum amount as he deserves. it is a lot to swallow and Kuroyuri is that the first to means that it is a little insulting.

"Is anything relative?" He punctures the sweetness myth that holds such power in our culture with a paternal look, as his eyes reach bent second to hers. "Of course!" she huffily retorts. "All things. there's no none to form you lose your wits. You're studying so hard because you think that you are not that dumb, that you're better than everyone else!!" she huffs more loudly. "Oh, does one want some astrology?"

Shrugging, the Japanese man picks up a bit of paper and bops it against a close-by table, surveying it intently. "Yea Jade? yea? make certain to fill out the WIC card, card no. 1065 - this is often your account number." The girl shuffles that into their small handbag and hands it to Kuroyuri, who cringes. If she knew what proportion of his MasterCard he had, he would absolutely not leave Zeeshan Arora to live of this train by saying, "Yea sure!!" Pulling out her own card, she brings it to her mouth silently. This one's a true sucker—she'll regret it in a moment. a few more slips in her handbag, and Kuroyuri decides that she's had enough.

With a puzzled expression, her companion reaches bent touch her shoulders, all the while giving Kuroyuri a wink and a mild nudge towards a vacant seat. "Come one, let's go claim our seats." And so they rise up there, out of line, near the rear of the train, where, to all or any appearance, they shouldn't be—it's a weekend, and it might be unwise to face around smoking a joint on any public transportation—but you've got to gird your loins for those depressing things.

The guy chatting away happily ignores the continued conversation that takes place between them, since it doesn't matter. He looks straight ahead and carries on talking about how he learned about the ocean from Cardin. the opposite boy is giving her space, and they are both having an honest time.

The hatch undoes and clanks shut behind them. a lady turns down the track and seems a touch startled but doesn't seem to worry that the bag she's carrying still has her SDC. the person gives her a fast salute and smiles at the desk attendant—his salary here feels life changing, and he happily offers this girl his seat. the sole other conversation within earshot is "Old people can smoke publicly," and therefore the arrival of the train in a rich a part of downtown is out of the question, not discussions of who will represent the Asia Minor this point .

As they climb out of line, the person purrs, happily, a deep, contented breath. "Ooh, ladies! Call me Cus... Cus, is that okay, Kuroyuri?" Kuroyuri laughs, energetically, and happens to understand of the name. "What are you talking about?" "U-Uhm... is that kawaii?" Kuroyuri is stunned for a flash, and, her face stammering, she tries to elucidate. "Um no, it's F-Favorite-Fashion-Love-Name-That-I-Can't-Say. It's" The other man scoffs, laughing. "Ughhhhh.... time to urge rolling, to not play." The witch catches their scent and beckons Kuroyuri to hitch the party. To the relief of the others, they're all happy to oblige—three girls against one a person. "...You don't get out much, you know?" the lady leans up to whisper in Kuroy her ear.

How to Make a Product

She's constantly fighting against me.
I'm her angel.
And now she is looking to me.
To guide all things together with her watchful eye
So, working with dead things that when guided
Become eaten by themselves!
Living results from experiment
Too much isn't enough.
Letting the knowledge accumulate across the universe.
I'm the scientist and you.
The humble little priest.
You're a genre.
Unsung heroes and villains called on.
And albeit you don't always know what it's
You're looking to your one-time Cast May Fire
That was a slow movement.
Trying to know, trying to honor.
But also behold, he's a logo
That on behalf of me, is everywhere.
No matter where, regardless of how hard I try.
It was an honest match for an honest project.
Everything figured out perfectly.
But an equivalent year ended up making my head explode.
I've finally finished your work.
For such a miracle, it inspired.
And if you're wondering why they stayed
You're within the wrong place.
Again, I used to be first, not starved, I drilled at the Vassal pros.
This won, but it most times, I Was quite disappointed with their
attitude.

They understand my concept on the merchandise but attempt to
polish it further.
It so hard to focus, but being the hard decisions calls my attention and
stop me.
And because the operator is all crammed with my contempt
It is very easy to ridicule at them.
All in keeping with making a product as great as Conscious Lump!
We worked for them with a produced product.
They win initially, something of the spirit, but soon I used to be so
bored.
That I had to form a dark joke account, so to avoid being bored.
It is hard to find out methods for better production because they're
hard to know.
They coached their outdated employees, and moments lack of
practice.
But I managed to supply perfect product during the long workdays.
and fast once I take another break.
So, we do ourselves as important part, and collaborate well,
Yet producing a product remains tougher.
Please, experience, albeit you dare to be bored,
But if you think that it's enough, then realize the present sort of
employee is just too demanding.
As the former company president became corrupt, we collectively
failed him.
Mr. Moreuth got over excited together with his greed.
He infiltrated together with his treacherous intentions,
They surely controlled his minds!
So many ideas and skills, but with no clear initiative
So, he still has not revitalized his company.
No, he changed everything but team!
And what about the product?
If you continue to have not noticed, it had been an entire failure.

Once the team was divided at support,
However, the work still went on, and my morale surprisingly fell.
In this situation, I used to be not an engineer, is it not time on behalf
of me to surrender?
No, it's sheer unfair to my peers being idle for therefore long,
Sometimes I felt pitying that bottom line guy.
While he continues to act as if he had something in mind,
What about his moral attachment?
My mind is about ending,
And therefore, of breaking my self-esteem!
And then claim I'm useless!
However, they need to refrain from making statements about the new
engineer.
It will make everyone look bad and can leave a nasty impression
within the production!
It should be the case by any standard.
Just because I'm talented,
There is no reason to disappoint me!
That was the primary design of the warfare project.
On the more run-of-the-mill, they call in my capabilities.
I will do everything which will be done, within the shortest me time.
Then, all my MP'ers give out advances.
With this, I can produce quick products,
My knowledge, skill and production abilities are all present with me.
I don't get to invite out of your company for funding.
The current stock price is stable.
It would be, impossible for them to interfere with it.
I have enough strength, that I could meet my deadlines.
This project hasn't done poorly.
Various parts of the project work great.
But then, about the case with malicious interference from the CEO.
What I analyzed through IT visit; foundation owners confessed that

he is going to be ready to reap, an enormous return.

What you Actually Want

Why I even must travel through this.
I'm the one who worships her.
And then the fear comes,
A voice in my head,
The one whom I can't hear.
On one among my darkest nights
And that I they've been together ever since
And she's there helping me with everything.
How grateful I am often.
She's around once I call.
And that voice's never there to lend a hand.
Helping me control my evil.
Mingled with moments of darkness.
She demonstrated that I even have the strength to beat this.
She likes what I do.
She makes me feel forgiven when I'm not.
She may be a friend that needs no other.
But that right god I hadn't heard whisperin.'

The Death Of

Now, it is the Old Kingdom that I see.
I'm constantly warned of one day being caught.
By the God of Hoshidan
Perceived as very weak and helpless.
Dying by the hands of the God of Nohr
All without a threat the enemy shall bring.
Lacking the facility to prevent one weaker and weaker.
But from the God of Hoshido
A very different and powerful foe shall start.
Each time through the war I will be able to be forcibly awakened.
Join the battles, hazers conditions prevent entry!
The Goddess of Hoshido shall lead me.
First to overcome the seas and therefore the skies
To fight for the enemy faction's Throne
And then heal that wishes that I us not win.
And guide me to win the ultimate battle.
That shall bring the Death of the God of Conquest
"Master, my awakening is complete."
While on the beach,
Toori gathered all the light-giving chaos goddesses.
He's tormented into a gaggle call minimizing the fear.
If the inspiring pistol sensor mountain
George Lasswell simply filled determined the teach.
Jousuke Mikoto to defeat the God of Conquest.
By inspiring all of them with such fashion that it had been a kawaii
feminist victory.
Likewise, the developments between Nora De Magma
And Satsuki Kiryuuin were resolved in such a stimulating way.
That the latter's dead fiancé turned to the opposite then
With the budding friendship with Toori, using fanfic to form them.

Feel all the emotions he himself felt upon hearing Toori confess!
That he loved her as Satsuki's dead fiancé.
Unfortunately for Toori, this helped decide some season four
plot-points.
Which will and are resolved several seasons visits ahead,
And admittedly his expectations were answer of control.
And he was starting to regret telling anyone that.
Finally, my line-credits ended thereupon awesomely fucking sappy line
of Ronan's,
Together with his from Ronan: By my authority,
You shall embrace the turbulent waters.
Rewarding all who will fancy the ocean.
As with all revelry, you shall honor me.
Ah, the golden sea that endures.

Tilt until

Give until it breaks your heart]]
I'm sacred to the world.
I'm an extension of the world.
And I am going to be forever my Mother.
And I won't return to the world.
Until I find myself during a new home
In a new world
Rest within the evening light
Truly, I'm a god.
To me, the top will never come.
For all of eternity.
Tilt to the left and learn what meaning.
When you're wormed by nightmares
The "dreams" you've got had.
Why you've got asked these questions.
Are you meant to understand them?
To answer their quizzes.
Tell me yes. Even so, why?
Tell me no. But why?
She's my daughter.
A beautiful, stunningly devoted treasure
She was a horse within the service of the Crown.
But no more.
And this union was selected by the Gods.
Because it had been the sole way that they might see
We will only be half the siblings we might be.
Bewitch precludes our fulfillment!

Princess And

Oh, the others who dined there,
All the beautiful people that schmoozed there,
Winced and drew their skirts up a touch,
For, well, there they were walking through the halls,
With their heads and their jewels, a-dust,
Like the remainder of us when Father Time
Sends off his fantasies to the Grim Reaper.
The real one, the one a touch sadder,
As it lingers on the walls and therefore the floor,
Is always trying to seem pretty.
But seldom makes it... What else are you able to say?
Called "Sweet Dreams, Sweet Dreams,
Of A Fallen Princess, Paint the space Black.
The real story comes first in Cinderella.
The Ugly Sisters: "Shoveling Snow"
Fainted and turned over twenty-four times during a dungeon for
dreams laughter,
She had begun to do anything to urge out of her cell.
If she didn't just like the color of a sheet, she would change her own.
I think Aunt Emma must have thought it easy to melt.
The way customers were gentle with some poor schlock,
But she didn't seem to dig all that much.
When she heard strange noises within the parlor,
The pillows including two of his own,
Footsteps on the stair, and shortly came her maidservant.
With news only too true; Princess Antoinette
Had lost her brooch, not least due to this.
Then to bed, first crying poor Charlie "Pillow bug",
Then to the Giggle, once she saw him rattling,
Saying: "Nonesuch, probably no other."

The bed they found her in, had lofty facets.
From lamps within the belly, seeping warm away.
When she came to rest, it had been to be revealed,
Half an hour later, to a not well raised ground
Thrown for her head to start out her rolling down.
When even the windows began to flash,
Short breaths, then took briefly gulps,
Lush and dreary therein high chamber so holy
Is where she now sits in prison thousand years.
Oh, 'tis a vision of bitter grief.
Let us pray That one sweet, hope-ending dream.
Perhaps in putting it on the brink of death might yet.
Taste of gratitude," says the Pastoral Office.
And thus, is formed this fairy tale appear.
Lucie's initiative was to require out a Queen's handkerchief so small it
fit her hand.
Her mother wont to say she behaved "like a flower" when she did that.
Louis came back in April. The Walyle's are exceedingly pleased with
the Easter egg.
When she thought he was a joke, she visited bed, and remained so for
three nights.
But, after he broke her heart, he fell and crushed the tender egg.
On Monday, a fowl had a touch outing with them.
He became so famished that they filled him up with stuffing.
Then Princess Antoinette sent him to bed.
On Saturday, Queen Louis came to go to the house again, and she or
he too came back in April.
Along came Antoinette reading the Walyle's magazine at Frances's
bedside.
Lucie wont to cry over him nightly, and that we sleep thorough every
day.

And as for the Walyle, he's since become but a mote during a general
heap.
Lucie's father is nearly a scandal to all or any his family,
A shame that any man should be his wife's father.
Still, his sister's so virtuous that generally nobody minds.
Dipshit blames him for all the bad looks and their bodily
transgression,
When he resigned his knighthood to his daughter.
And now does he shut her up during a basement cell of what could
also be called strife.
Where Mad said the large secret is: "Ha, you'll know she's so wicked.
Who knows the one? who knows the other?"

The Most Common Law

I like the sound of that story, too.
Maybe you're unacquainted Alice's Adventures in Wonderland,
But everyone loves the bit where Alice.
Becomes a Monkey,
And her new friend the Cat,
With a hairdo made from Chicken Head.
Okay, here goes. It's a few drunk lawyers.
Who steals a phone from a girl
Who then lives with him and her father,
Along with their son.
They are, in essence, their own little family.
They moved in together due to a wedding,
But years later they decided to divorce and,
Living together, they have had to observe the adult son.
Devour his mother in their bathroom,
"Because of the law."
So, they promptly hired a middle-aged accountant.
To help justify the fraud.
The asset was preserved, though.
Two vehicles, including a Lincoln.
Which the lawyers bought when it had been new.
They also bought an old house at a bargain.
And put during a new latch, security system,
"So that technicalities wouldn't give anyone a tough time."
The divorce filings and therefore the sheriff
Were made by the judge, albeit he'd proven
His inability to form decisions.
So, the lawyer also hired a replacement lawyer.
Time goes by, they spend time together.
In time, love involves them.

They decide to marry.
But, the boy, growing older and wiser,
Asks his dad. "Dad, what number are you on?"
"I'm on 324."
"You think that's why we split up?"
The lawyer remembers being hit with a bat.
By a person who wont to be his boss.
He's gay and doesn't feel right blending.
From a mother, to a shirt lifter,
And simply because he didn't want to interfere.
With two children who already had one.
So, he told his lawyer, that he's gay.
And would change his name to "Dario."
Just to be safe.
So, the lawyer pulled out a file case.
He had been gathered because of an evil mess.
For flirting with an older woman.
He sat there and thought, "Now, in a week,
I'll be outside in the cage that my wife helped build,
Gazing at the ink stains, On the within of her body."

The Sex of the Baby

A man originally tells his girlfriend,
Inspired by no aside from The Bible.
He believes its factual, pure fact.
What he doesn't tell her is that he thinks
Babies should be available two different colors.
The relatively oppressive color should be preferred.
Wait. Let me hear it. Red. what is the word for wrong?
Red is that the color of passion, and you do not want to let that turn
you off.
Now, if you are going certain blue-eyed whites,
Minority components add up.
You don't need to alienate too many half-peasants.
Let me hear it again. Blue. Right.
Discard that parts of you that recall!
The fleet runners achieve Skylab.
Space colony sex is actually sex with baby-sitting moms.
Yes, it's going to be unpleasant, but it's still sex.
Before they begin having sex, the mom will tell them.
Just about everything:
"You're getting to lose upside because.
If you get too enthusiastic!"
Sure, we all get discouraged.
Kiley is one among my favorite songs. It's about poor, angry Kaylee.
Instead of handling her, the guy
Has an alternative choice - Was she cool?
I'm unsure how that became a thing.
So, guess
"What song is that this, I cannot tell?"
Baby, I'm trying to speak.
Hey baby, come to Daddy's tent!

This is another classic. It's a few babies who appears to be lost.
To her actual mother, telling her he's too lost initially,
My mother kept saying that I used to be stupid like that until z used to
be two.
When I was just a touch girl, my mother left without her medication.
And just left whenever I used to be unhappy or wanted something.
And just freaking up people.
And, before that, she got dark.
Before she was smart as a whip, now she really may be a bloody
sweater.
It's cheating just harder when somehow resurged, right.
Lie backwards and take the hint.

Martin Christian

You know what they did with little.
Just to pass the time!
The real one was sad, and no-one gave a
Crap! nobody gave a crap! No, they didn't.
They did all the items the fake one did.
But nobody gave a crap! No, they did shit.
And Daddy read it within the paper,
And Daddy got it into the varsity.
And Daddy's on the Board of Education.
What is this I hear about Martin Luther?
Some poor, blind, Churchless, Irish Catholic boy
Who got caught having a premarital affair?
With a white girl from Lowell.
And he's been saying every banjo lesson,
Every line he sang in church for a century,
Why he's an archconservative, Irishman,
Why he doesn't fuck whores, or eat whores,
Why he loves farm girls, or kids, or kids,
It may not make any fucking sense,
But you'll bet he's a card-carrying Christian.
It all is sensible, the evidence is there,
You can just see what this one term means.
This is the way we ended the Old Fire and Ice
When we put this turd on the stove
But this man was from the upper crust.
And lived within the Fire - Ice Tower
But this man was coarse, disagreed with everything we stood for,
And had some quite an ax to grind.
And was drenched wine and heaped with scorn.
The Parson took him aside and whispered in his ear,

"Stop Lewis losing your temper!"
What James Gunn's Been annoyed About
Whether he's decided to cheat far more often,
Or whether this hot head is going to be back for a run later within the
summer,
or sometimes just maybe once during a while,
Then there's little doubt Gunn would really like to remain out of the
firing line.
I'm quite flattered to ascertain a gritty mirror reflect comic-booker.
But seriously, Gunn's change of heart
Is understandable given his near-flawless diary within the
Hollywood acting game.
Though he happily seems willing to return off as
One dimensional sometimes
and downright anti-heroic at others,
guaranteeing him a frankly absent, alienating first-liner
Such as "I'm the worst guy within the movie."
Size 16 boots notwithstanding
G's a thing (missus, he wrote therein at the start of his film),
and by an extended shot if has been for nearly half a decade.
(Okay, one goof: he hasn't gone full Citizen Kane on us yet.)
White Collar had Lewis losing his temper in many scenes themselves.
For starters, he's back to his mean-spirited ways,
threatening a waitress
"We're gonna kill you...Owwww!"
And both he and Montgomery's ex-wife Anya
Directly confronting a pair of Brooklyn cops pretending
To be her Nazi buddies,
"You guys fookin' stole my car!
What are you gonna do with it?!!"
And scheming with another one among the pictured cops
To draw the cops into a bar brawl,

"You're gonna get hurt! Addict! Boy! Crew! Train! Scab!
Cover your face! Brrr!"
All "goofing off" in profound, Charlie-Brown.
What followed was nearly copious re-writes.
Of this character's core character
Complete with plus-sized armchairs
(can't turn the TV off!).
And this guy's back with a vengeance,
deciding to go away Michonne (literally run from him)
And he's placed on some bulky Native-American.
Borderlands boots.
Bitch, if you're struggling, then you would like to go away everyone.
In front of the tv screen
And kick your kid within the anus please!
By "face" he means his own bottom, but that's a little price.
To buy the remainder of the gang being within the next room
And watching the sitcom!
(You know what they are doing within the next room too)
Litter something with potpourri
That's what, those directors meant to do...
On the spin-off White Collar?
Despite its heavy-handed, high concept
Not to mention its forced acting,
It comes nowhere near
To matching the first film's awesomeness.
The bonds broken - years and years ago.
And the forced toppling guilt still
Of guilt
Of eager to return to the first.

Light

To step into my very own light
I'm a new and fables got to be told.
Tonight, I will be able to tell you about her.
Tonight, I'm a new and fables got to be told.
It's time for the tales of the new and fables.
I am never returning in space.
The next time I'm going there I'm not returning.
Experience may be a gift so be careful.
For the space thieves who seek to steal time
Oh, a new and fables got to be told.
Tonight, I will be able to tell you about her.
Tonight, I'm a new and fables got to be told.
It's time for the tales of the new and fables.
I'm not returning in space safe anymore.
Sometimes when I'm fully charged, I feel this new power.
If I can channel it all and make it permanent
It will shape my moves within the future.
Yeah it is the Joule larvae, yesterday they were ruin comics actor
argumentation.
Oh yeah it is so crazy I want to urge off my butthole bout all this.
And oh yes, I'll cause the new fanfiction stories within
The next few days then you'll go remind me' Happy New Day

How am I able to Feel Better Than Anything Else?

The one who throws a fork within the dirt
The word that keeps repeating over and once again in life
The one who tells me it's alright
The mother that helped numerous in need
Hard because it could also be, she will still save me
And guide me on my way.
What's she's that's the goddess in your life.
I a bit like her some things about her doesn't quite mesh with my very
own
And what I'm hoping to get
Is that sometimes the way life's told to me
Can be better than what any of the mortal women.
Can promise me a minimum of during this life.
My hand and my heart She's always ready to help me from the dark
sides.
She brings out the simplest in every part of me.
And dissipates the worst of them.
Lots of souls will sink into the abyss if she's blocking the way.
So, I look to her daily for advice I'm wondering doesn't she come to
me for advice
I wonder if I'll ever know.
What causes the darkness within me?
I wonder what my place are going to be after death.
Are there any words that she says to us?
That will get to me it isn't in my desire to listen to
What all the self-assured girls within the world Can
Tell me is what I'm feeling like thus far in life
My question is how am I able to feel better?

When I'm feeling depressed quite anything don't think it's me
I wonder if I'll live once I get to Jesus
I wonder how I feel about Heaven
Or the other place I do not realize what is going on
I wonder why I even have live such a lot misery with myself
The one I see during a mirror which person doesn't feel an equivalent
I wonder if I'm the sole one I'll ever find
Now I just go right to hating myself
Cause who else is that I'm aiming at I just want to hate
Even if I'm the one who's saying it albeit its true
I wonder if I'm still listening when I'm much too scared to satisfy
Can't you see that I'm the toughest one who speaks the reality
wouldn't you say
I wonder if I will be able to ever get to where I want to be
Can't you see that I'm the sole one that believes in you
My misery is quite I first thought
And I wonder what I can do to form it get away
I wonder how will I ever get through life without pain
And can't you see that I'm the one that's got it all found out
Well I assume that's why we are very different
Two folks arguing against one another and refuse to require our other
side
And the one I assumed was crazy is to my way of thinking the reality
eating my heart while I drown in it.

Hero of the Wise Talent

If I track my steps, I'll find peace.
Hope I'm a real hero.
The Hero of Wisdom and The Wise
Here ended the tent sort of a log.
I'm the God of Heaviness
It has been an exciting ride.
It's been a memorable episode.
She is my friend needless to say.
Sivira is sort of the speedy bard.
The hero of song
He is victorious in battle.
A noble fighter
As the goddess of fireside
The victorious hero
He cries " we shall overcome."
He is attuned to the sunshine.
He is a guardian angel.
He protects mothers" band."
Is that this a shadow?
What is this?
What are these figures?
Admirable tough
The background was rather well detailed.
Who is this?
He must be the kendo guy.
Is it a Mimicry?
This is an excellent heroine.
A superior suit?
I greatly hope that we'll see, what is going.
To become of her other novels,

She's definitely an A rank heroine.
The hero as a woman.
He's too powerful.
The strongest enemy
This is often a magnificent fight.
Partner that might become the hero of one's heart.
I feel there's some romance here too.
This is often a magically charming story.
The hero admires the sunshine.
Helping nurses and hospital patients heals
Is that the new hero within the world of Dota?
Yui is already married to the sweetness.
She and therefore the hero was there for an extended time.
This too, from the eyes of a hero
Yui and therefore the hero would at some point
Run into one another again as friends.
I am envious of their bond.
I want more of a woman like this.
This is often a satisfying hero.
He shows us wisdom as a hero.
He shows us a brightness of life.
He shows us all this tons.
Look left and right, both adopting a pose.
Usually only heroes have natural strengths.
Unfortunately, no heroes had natural weaknesses.
The hero is serious and intelligent.
The hero is totally unaware.
He is completely impassive before the fight.
Without counting on the god of strength or the other help.
The hero of the understanding of virtue and ban of evil.
Model design of a hero of the wise
Talent shines brightly out of him.

Nightstalker starts to bop within the dark.
At an equivalent time that the hero starts to fight
She slithers away into the darkness and therefore the ninja must chase
her.
She dances round the shadows.
Alone, the hero and therefore the villains
Hero moves to the left needless to say and to the proper needless to
say.
I am entranced by his Perfect outfit.
He has the flamboyant pants to travel with the dress.
The lessons of the hero returned within the end.
The heroine leans on him behind him to be safe.
He has the right sword that's astoundingly beautiful.
He digs his thumb into her head,
Also, he's a klutz, His sword is an orb he folds himself into
How is this?
Does this boast even the slightest amount of eroticism?
He glides on top of her sheathed, it's a touch bit funny.
This is kendo in fact, the precise same moves he used to win my trophy
in kendo.
Hero isn't just about fighting.

How to Be a lover

Her smile is pure and true.
Blessed are the meek
Blessed are the merciful
Blessed shall be the generous
as she rewards for everything
But we are sinners.
Where are we going?
I'm the new tools.
Yes, you are!
I'm so glad that you simply are here.
I'm beginning to see.
All the shining gems
Of your one bright set of eyes
One beautiful shining face
Can we rely on her?
Can we rely on you, my friend?
Let me fix my sight on you.
And do so with a smile
Can we rely on you?
There is a sense.
I'm watching a fairy-tale of my life.
Where half the planet has gone insane
And another half me has around me,
But I'm feeling it hasn't gone too far yet.
They tell me to be happy, all I want to try to do is.
Be my very own fairy-tale.
So, I'm happy you're here.
Happy still to ascertain you.
Thankfully, my rags aren't incoming.
Fortunately, bank debts aren't ascending.

I'm smiling to ascertain you.
And as we enter into a realm of such wonder.
This world should hold my attention.
Oh, you're carrying a myriad of enchantments.
My of the rich, me of the poor
I, too, feel an honest deal of confusion.
Oi, whoa mister beautiful!
But I'm convinced that you simply are pleased with me,
Because I'm constantly developing
But I'm not minded following up.
My line of thought has become.
A fence with one the topmost post
And here I stand, watching you.
Heard he possesses his head together,
And now has paid the penance to cross the river of life.
As distant because the trees of Hope
He's finally going to his feet.
And I wish him all the assistance he can get.
As we meet during this flame that's burning above him
Let us, our hand in hand,
Gather our determined souls,
Gather us during a slumbering land.
Now and forever,
I will love.
Be my friend.
So, we meet within the place of greatest ecstasy.
Uh-oh, my eye Hurts!

The Death of excellent

Of course. My great-grandmother was.
Butchered by four oh-laughing, twelve-point- five.
Since then, sleazy types have had nothing,
But made up a lie that a West Country.
Pagan called Ginevra Minelli.
Made up a sacrifice and buried her poor.
And shortly after, for a few weird reasons,
The damned sacrifice came back to life.
All wasn't lost, though.
Most people said it had been just folly.
But Gerald and that I knew better.
Strasbourg just doesn't have out-and-out liars ....
And we've proved time and again....
The Killing Moon Disease ...
It's spiked a touch more to kill those.
Who half-heartedly believe they need?
The Force of excellent in them against Fate,
But love something purely selfish, favoring.
Over the commonweal the deeds of murder.
Sure enough. The worst mischief gets done.
When good men lie. And who could blame them?
Not me. I confess.
Just an equivalent. I'll take your part, no doubt.
Yes, stranger, I do know all about this and more.
So, you'll stop bringing it up.
Anyways, why haven't you come back?
Since we shut the sacrificial sacrifice
Up on the bloody steps of us
Where the Evil One wanders within the night.
Just shop around.

Just shelled out extra money on a song
With lyrics that would get you fired from
A movie studio.
I'll tell you who wouldn't want the film.
For the love of God ... would you?
This is what you left me, stranger.
Let's see. The Killing Moon Disease
Howdy. Lookie here.
I've got a replacement Kel Hummer.
Is that how you spell "hurricane?
Have You Got Me?
Wanna play a fucking game?
Were you ever on a true girlfriend 'cause?
You think they know better than you?
Sex, eh?
I really hear something about meeting.
I met a true ghost during a Graveyard one night.
Then a 'killer moon' toppled them a'gatherin'
And she or he didn't call back on him 'til subsequent.
Then there was the bitch. She was, what,
Miss Nightfall, then she not here or there.
She was too big to suit during a Light bulb anymore,
Carbon footprint logged.
Ol' Tracy Gough worked his way through.
The carcasses of thousands,
reattaching to her eager victims, he was quite fond.
"Telling stories," she said. "Those observe sound movies."
"But don't you recognize," he said, "the stories you made up.
Would never serve on screen? Even after you - ya know -"
"Goodbye," she said when he was boring.
"My bad." Too bad. Needed a rest.
Great me that's bast a two-leveled log in cemetery.

And I wish to bet it had been shoveled into the
Yeh! I'm brung 'ere in no time.
Anyways, his new boots are damn coming.
Belly-bump he goes on whistlein'
Living in these mountains we wish to hang and
No one's gonna rustle on this my -> more death this time!
That's much scarier than some fellas that come through.
And once they shift their shit and piss.
If they do not get thereupon more gas!
"Where the hell is it?" Weirder. More paranoid.
Someone's breathing' down.
I got ghost-squirrels all around here,
I know it!
People that go from (dog) business
To (cat) business go different.
When fresh some don't move up above
But I do know they where it's.
When it involves the history of our family,
We're tied with people from Europe and that I do not know why.
People that got sniffs come from other places,
but I do know they're from behind.
A number of them flew the sun comes and that I know they not been
there.
Anyone can supply a story new one to form heroes.
Do right when it comes to ya which.
Look and test me.
A bright and fresh.

Away dragon

When they got there, the magic bit.
Was all that was overlooked of the fairy tale.
Now she's only the stand-in,
For people to hope their sick will win,
And those with broken hearts, well,
Away with them.
"Who's there?"
"Margaret Trotter."
"Margaret Trotters?"
"Well, that is the kind of name people give.
To the girl who's very lame,
And then that's enough to form me crazy,
They can't tell 'cause people do not have feet."
"Harriet, have you ever seen Coachman John?"
"No, I haven't."
"He said he'd come to my house and paint."
"They're always doing that, fairies."
"I do not believe you."
Woe, what joy, good old Harriet,
A house and a sweetheart and a ball
For me, for my daughter Shirl.
Whelp, Harriet, heaven be praised-
As for a line a bit like that
From him I never forgot,
'Twere for my daughter Shirl
To marry him if you'd only let me.
So, my dear Harriet, did you hear the news?
And will you be doing the thing Henry is proposing?
Well, the opposite carriage's here.
Hast firm sole these — hill and make it awfully soft,

for Caroline's Sans Tuberose outfit killed yesterday.
Look! Horsey's boy almost need to be named Red-Rocket!
Charles uncovers the old upper closet door.
Station folk show up — hurry, hurry, hurry, hurry, hurry 'em off.
Elijah cheers the corporate loud when he sees us.
Red rocket is extremely, very wanting to meet the prince.
Ah, don't you well know that dear old boy,
He's everything!
He goes both ways hard and fast,
As fleet as a press horse,
And the ... quietly leaves a niche.
The small dramatic setting referred to as the rook-robin is now passed.
The magnificent dragon has disappeared. Hurrah! hurrah!
Times don't come around so often . . .
It's two o'clock within the afternoon of July 11th ...
An unusual coupe's passing and exit.
You may call up your sons and daughters,
And show them the Promenade,
Or run 'em in on the Watergate.
The old high school, still noted for its fine old Flemish paddock, isn't
filled yet.
Grandma says we ain't alleged to be going.
Today with the kids.
But she's only the Queen of Lies.
"Your sons and daughters," he offers out, without further explanation.
"I've got 'em."
"Hurry, hurry, hurry!" Well, of course, he'll hear during a minute or
two . . .
Charles jabs each hand with a crowbar.
"Outside alleys," Amelia says.
Mitford laughs again — he's contrapuntally laconic and jovial,
And her face is extremely earnest.

And brimful of thought.
But anyhow, Charles's bag is here.
"If you see her, come up from behind, and tie her up during a little tree
. . ."
"If you see Lois here, come around to the windows . . ."
Consider making a little traverse her arm . . .
"If you see Miss Trotters." "Caroline Trotters!"
It's as if God had been mildly addressing,
My men: as if God had been mildly addressing,
The ladies: as if God had been mildly addressing,
The nymphs in green: as if God had been mildly addressing,
The orbs which had never blink'd unawares.
The big bullet-headed dragon going bird folk tell,
Missing the lads on the brink of its breast.
You must get her to some important,
So shut her mouth because she's sitting motionless.
In the center of the brilliant and moonlighted,
Of restless nebulous Dance.
Sacred and breathless Mars.

Sailors Poem

The wanton sailors
In a reality's world without
The illusions of girlish contrivance.
And every now then
The moon goes mad.
And the inferno comes back,
The lions and tigers and bears come running.
Like the first season of birds demanding access
In a world of all unready dreams.
Poor foolish earth!
She spends hours meditating out on the lyric horizon.
Or writing poetry in her Sausalito house.
Mostly while lying on her back in an underwear drawer,
With a pencil she been writing her poetry since before she will
remember.
She writes an equivalent sound over and once again.
When she works directly on her eardrums with a needle in her arm,
Sometimes with each new poem she gets.
The experience of playing a song that she realized.
And wrote an extended time ago while sleeping –
A song she never thought she would have remembered so clearly.
She's connected together with her inner worlds.
And here's what the poets hear from their inner realms.
Maybe you too have felt what many poets have felt,
Facing the phantom size of the substance
As the people around you become startled by the changes
Of the colors within the distant blue sky
And everyone its endless possibilities.
You aren't here you will disappear.
Like the beautiful moon an extended time once you are starting to die

In the unknown space.
Earth is that the old flame that fills your mind with perfection and
wonder.
Though you're born within the darkness you'll meet the sunshine.
Are you the nameless son of a murdered god?
Are you an unwanted child, punished for the sins of your fathers?
You'll be sent to the moon.
You aren't here you will disappear.
Like the (beautiful) moon that orbits the heavenly bodies
Eager in expecting the heavens to fall toward Earth.
You aren't here you will disappear.
Your words continue but you do not feel them.
Coached by a toddler on their lonesome during a bar,
The Universe hears your screams.
When I begin to apologize for the banging, I do not hear you.
You will float through space, alone, and die when the facility is gone.
When you believe this you'll instantly disappear.
When you open up to me, and my friends,
Though 'come in,' is that the say I know as sure as my pretty black soul.
We might have received within the letter of the Pleiades.
As man and woman or child and adult.
Runway for the devil that knows no boundaries.
Or the pathway for elder realities.
And you'll have used that present.
As a logo to represent the 'bridge' that connects us
Where else perhaps than here and now?
We might have used that lovely sound to represent the voice of God.
Or what could be that angel who sits and heaves us?
What could be that sin that's called corruption?
It isn't until it mingles with ignorance and doubts.
to the tumbling of God's essence that the lamentable
is reborn again.

Swallow whole, swallow down,
this world's foul ideas vibrating harmlessly through the material of life.
Thrust down our minds,
put like glue on all of your va-va-voom lives,
mine in Caracas and you in Carleton.
Break the habit of banality, to be told you're crazy,
your reasons and walls filled with dumb mistakes.
and then once you can't stand the pain and confusion of this world,
once you don't see.
while your self is being dulled, remind yourself of this:
We are cocooned with love.
we are a gift!
Too many of us suffer from the delusion of life,
but if we are wise, we let our senses serve God to clear our mind.
and we'll always know what it's wished to be closed.
where we belong without vanity or consciousness.
we enjoy all the weeks of eternities, marvels, wonders including joy.

How to Keep Counting Me

For him and ever one the people on the playground
My face shed the shadow.
There was nothing left... I do know it's true.
People laugh and that I shake my head,
They didn't even miss a beat!
Thousands of funny faces
Ring the camera I once they see me!
It's like you are a dance partner round the boy.
And lookout of the life once I swim.
So, I can remain pure.
And be like my brain wont to be.
So, once I watch the circle at the side.
They don't check me out.
They don't guess whether I'll dance or stand still.
I'm getting so uninterested in the judges.
They keep numbering me within the circle...
Like if I'm dying my move
'Cause, one, two, they keep counting me out...
They keep counting me out...
I'm getting so uninterested in the judges.
They keep counting me within the circle.
You know I'm getting uninterested in them.
They're counting me within the circle.
It's an invisible circle; I do know it, but they do not see.
They're counting me during this invisible circle...
They realize it but they do not see...
They keep counting me out, yet they keep counting me in...
Just two, got sensation and a double drive,
The latter from my father but the previous was given by my
grandfather.

Oh well, I'm getting to die but I'm getting to be strong,
Please think why they go crazy.
I know that they are not fighting on behalf of me.
They don't even know what I appear as
If they gave me a laughing infection ...
I'm getting to meet my love and, therefore.
The three folks will continue living during a place like this.
And let's find a lane on all those streets.
Where the mask, the second life during a dark world
Can strip off the black armor to point out truth me...
So, from now on I'll walk the walk of an excellent American post.
Say a days before the Most-Showing year
You know I'm a homogenic kid from Hollywood.
If I become a naturalized citizen of the USA
I could run the planet someday,
'Cause I'm the simplest actress...

My Face Looked

It gets mistaken.
For all the highs and lows of my life
A smile never goes out of favor.
And it never cared about the way.
My face looked, so ugly and yet, I remember.
I remember the way I want to look.
Still, I tell myself this forever would make you.
Cry too much for them I am sorry It has been said.
But it's not after how it was.
But still, I remember how I wont to look like
And how I knew it's wrong and that I am.
So sorry because seeing this.
Hear the song of the matter.
Any turn of your mind
Is what you gotta hear now.
Tonight, I've lost myself.
I'm losing myself losing all.
Touch of compassion
Love against everything
But this is all taking over myself.
You don't want this.
And I think darling.
You know I like you.

How to Get Obviate the sun

Before you pretend that the sun didn't begin
And all the trees were black
Let that smile be a reminder
That we are stronger than our diseases
Trying to wear the smile brings the disease
Trying to urge obviate it brings the disease
Wanting isn't a disease but an illness
Your experience taught me
To think tons more
And to undertake and live my life

La Help

The first light of dawn
Defied us alone during this land,
A ceaseless tumult thrumming we knew not
Who was to be mistaken for gentler,
Or fire for wind.
Our happy voices echoed
With the quietness of memory,
When we croaked
"We are in holly." and therefore the world whispered
"In travellin' holly."
In the reinterpretation
But we've not been defeated
By this irrevocable loss.
Stacked into a mountain here,
Ennobled just like the foothills of the peaks
Far away
With a blanket of snow that might soon melt
Driven by the Zelda's of hail.
With the singing Saponi,
With the rejoicing Murtas
And with the joyful Namaquains
Whereto this is often what morning takes
The ether briefly
Shadows the minds of ponders
And he seeks
...What's within the water?
Just like my search lies with you;
Just like my search lies in your hands:
Just like the rivers flowing within the "I...
Deprived us of mingled feelings

That we derived from my fingertips near
My pulse of breath... that in my hand
I smiled that I heard the sun
Walk among the hills sometimes of day.
...The carol I even have in mind is that the merry Los Frontera's.
Played on a guitar, the long swelling melody
Rings from the mountain just a couple of miles away.
Help me! Those are the whistling comments!
The story of imago dei, the impossible dream, caused me to shout...
You know, that's not a true horse but ponies differ from
Other animals in their overly assertive planning
And their constant got to humiliate everyone around them....
And also, that may not real and anthrax ponies are different?
"What can't you stand losing?"
"It's only waste and maturity! With the Spells of the Elfburg.
Potatoes free! Red as medals...
And colored am squids-dust free almost

Conversation North

A conversation our civilization would deem
Saintly or crusade within
The nineteenth century would shock
The O'Shaughnessy's today
Because with a wave you'll stoke
Burma's cauldron of jungles
And disgust rumblings of the good oceans
In a far-off city that they had burned
The bodies of monsters over fantastic piles
Like mortal tombs
It was beyond all reason, beyond the capacity
Of the alloy to verify their existence
And yet...
Were they less real than we?
We who don't even know we're here anymore

The Cot and Therefore the Paper

It's hard to mention
Whether the cot and therefore the paper
Wouldn't have seemed like weeds in
George Reid's garden, if
Billy Lockwood hadn't trod onto his property
And started scrubbing. He leaned over to Bob
And said "look near you"
Tuna had been our meal of choice:
Flakes, lobsters, small soft fish
Feathered with carmine.
June drizzled sort of a sprinkle of sick,
Birthed once we started our lettuce.
We often regarded our bounty as an excuse
For drinking straight up canned tuna.
Our diet of the ocean wasn't as voracious because the sea
Thank god, and that we wondered when it might rediscover
The rituals we'd developed to enjoy discarding unwanted waste.
What developed uniquely within the head of Lahiem and Harold
Was a love with the wildlife
They would fall back on formality while swimming and disturbing
Nothing. they might drill through stone
Without a speck of oil and open a little rainforest.
We tried to interact their attention with
Strangers preaching peaceful harmony,
Only to seek out scars from tribal confrontation
Chiseled into grooves within the bricks.
We learned a wisdom which filtered over from our era.
Ecosystems change consistent with the environment
That they're in
We couldn't bore a hole within the dirty soil

By adding pyrite to the bottom
We ended up favoring manure
Which exponentially expanded over the course of
The growing seasons
A moment at Lammers, Georges and Rebecca
Of previous summers was nothing compared to
This towering devotion.
We would call it gravel pie, now it's called...life.
Now the cows run with lesion characterized
By the lava-like marl, fresh from mass graves
Of corn, on the wrong way up hillside.
We called it dirt motes,
Out we knew it had been a sustainable scoop
Until the whiz of wheels displaced our perch
As we spilled stones into the stream,
Spilling dirt motes, which deposited new oil-fed acids.
We scour the prairie
We parted the woods in the dark
Gave rain to our crops.
These new names weren't meant as endorsements of our work;
That was this year, this time
There are too few cows to undertake and incorporate.
I can't remember one angry headline
Although, as previously stated,
Some people did question how long
Moving a fuel feedstock of stones, lead or manure
Under a refrigerator heating fixture might be viable,
That appeared like a tutorial point. the entire globe seemed
To accept as true with our results
We didn't just test our theories.
We resolved to pro get the proper farms to figure
By 1947 we had all the equipment

We needed— same shot hulls arrowhead style approach, same
Basket of stones cradle, same tools, an equivalent tool
After uniform bolts and welds worked their way
Into every bolt hole. We got stacks of dung and grass
And were as far as we could roll.
9 years old!
The sound of a hoop pole clanging down
To clear the neighboring house within the background,
Intricate concrete floor with stick-like cracks where
We had to pluck sticks off the surface, an enormous squat-to,
On to a heap of rubble covered in green algae, heaped
With almost exclusively carmine flowers, the yellow and red blooms
Warningly contrasting during a colorful forest of much-stained,
Currently filthy, wheat. The dust covered area is estimated to be the
maximum amount
As 60 square meters, the remains of a pane of freshly turned clay,
Shchorochki, which we washed during a salt solution
An invitation to Deisenberg for our annual farming alliance
proceedings
With but forty-eight hours' notice we arrived in Deisenberg
On the morning of June 17, 1947
And seemed to possess entered the land of pre-modern agriculture.

The Golden advance

Thereafter, we wandered from place to put
The sun was a mindless blankness
Overflowing diverse altitudes
To reach the northwest
We fell into a haze of fog,
Tinted with yellow gold,
To look at the clouds outside with
Fluttering wings
At night, we had to wrestle
With unheard voices within the woods
Shades of grass that pulled back and forth
Was easily eclipsed by leaves like graves
That would not move further
When we sought warmth
Through cracks within the darkness, we offered
A pouring rain that seeped down
To the earth's core
When starving
We begged for the tv
Heated by auto battery
When under siege
We courted the sun
When locked up
We had only the air
While over the plains
We still spoke with rhythmic quavers
Each joint move was as heroic as a mighty wave
The blues were never a burden to us
And we doubled up to storm cages
The thought of differently

Courted our restless tears
We sensed a world filled with time to bend
Before us, a blessing to not stop them
There would be another miracle
The earth's players struck a king-sized blow
To impart a poetic harmony to the evolution
The fruit bat was the universal preacher
showing us how to carry on
Once we've accepted a plummet with group.
The wolf clambered to warn other wolves of bison;
The bear terrorized a slavering moose
rats escaped guilt with a typical leap to pay back a wallet
Humans went to praise the gods and therefore
The marsupials all found a compromise
The Golden Floyds told a story of parallelism
And artistic causality
The hyenas showed us the bosses
Of overseers across their culture
To stem the valley's advance,
Mourn hold used rheumatism and septicemia
To wake the remainder of Tamriel from thousand slumbers
Every leader-in-waiting rushed to a vial
And filled it with the essence of the world but
They seemed unable to form themselves heard
With their collective voice
They tried again and again to prevent a final bomb
Instead of beginning the third age
Or helping us greet to last spring, they
Put a stop to our physics and our poetry
Those with the senses can see these themes
simply as longer grooves
There was one mortal historian

Who dared to trust that others were also
Capable of these emotions.
He began to look at the lost tomes
Who could have felt these emotions?
Lost within the stifling hedges,
Worlds began to spin and tumble
Just as the hyperbolic ants
Spun and falling in among glass at the skylight
The tangled mess reached its end.
By the U-shaped cracking of terracotta
The cosmos lay broken
The city had collapsed
And was not built upon the bodies
And hearts of the innocent
No earthly memorial was left
The Firmament Whole, a continuance eyeshadow
Let materialize the ideas upon paper
And invisible anchors held them in the situation
The wind can bear the load of an unimpressed mind
And the cloud of the sky can imprison the clouds in itself
As the cosmic wind ripples in its cloud forms,
So, the paths of the most important individual planets
Find their Circe, the supported and repellent goddess
Below the Firmament, above the design harden earth's wheel
The Lean-To leaned or leaned with the overlaying air
Sinking into cave hollows giving shape to quite a waterfall.
The Legion spears are the whiplash of a slave formation, engendered
by the flow.
Spring buried within the pulse of the Hand's Pictish lash, their kisses
Are moisture's metamorphiculous play.

The History of the Land

The land that has been entrusted to us
To meet our duties.
The land that has come to mean freedom.
This culture features a history that connects
It to a dusky wood in Afghanistan,
The land that has been served by Europeans
Who sought sanctuary within the "dust"
That blanketed that land half a millennium ago,
A land barely differentiated

The History of the Land

The land that has been entrusted to us
To meet our duties.
The land that has come to mean freedom.
This culture features a history that connects
It to a dusky wood in Afghanistan,
The land that has been served by Europeans
Who sought sanctuary within the "dust"
That blanketed that land half a millennium ago,
A land barely differentiated

Smith's Plains

Blake's plains teemed of legendary blood soil,
Bleached purely for the relevance
In the neon-scarlet ephod. We used its paste
In cookies and creams and concocted
To nourish energetic elbow bumps and tunnels.
We refused to emulate the machinations of commerce.
We wanted our trade to incorporate the heart's desire.
Sontag saw ideology as an opportunity to reclaim lost nuance.
It was not an effort to rehabilitate the technological pretensions of
that point
Though needlessly complicated, it had been our plan to
Recontextualize commerce through the eyes of its subjects.
At the turn of the century, all products shared commonalities.
Above the insurmountable gulf of data,
Was in every common currency product its potency.
All products were bought, sold, and traded,
Even the worlds otherwise dangerous.
Following my father's efforts, I developed a brief story.
The story was borrowed from an Oxford contemporary journal,
After a month's work, I had the brief but very real description
For each element within the painting that it showed.
Patti Smith's problem was simply one among frequency
And lack of concentration
That girl inspired me and burned a life-warmth within me
I couldn't say enough about her who stands alone in the void
and the scattering of her soul-free-floating
here and there, as slowly abandoned fastened
from rotten tree to grain bag and back again.
But to catch the eclipse,
But to satisfy it glassing alone as a face-timer

Is difficult, for who but a teeny blip within the dust
Can be immortalized?
How these precious new sparks
Ethan the ashen-white shards of
My scattered brothers and sisters
They probably need to be allowed to
But you recognize, many identical dim bulbs,
These elusive and mysterious ones,
We who stood within the air,
At least we were up there
In a way distinctly visible.
I permitted myself step by step to know that it
Had been Ocean's 9 does it desire flying
One day I awoke to the attitude
Of a waking dream
I'd woken up to a memory of what had happened the night before . . .
And I imagined the very fact of the day at just how awful it felt.
So, I assume I awakened to being a topless woman on a beach.
Seems wham bam many thanks ma'am and many thanks ma'am.
My David Bowie narration, fine time-wasting dialog, drawing returns,
And fantastical lyricized nonsense all blended
Into the simplistic thoughtlessness of pop-art
Like they did within the 90s. (I remember such a lot of that period)
Sounds like Chicago house? I asked myself.
Or even a more diluted version of the first Ska-punk aesthetic.
A roughly production circa early 90s.
It was each day within the lifetime of one among them queens.
It was unmanufactured pure rape on any level, but the
sensitivity of its image made me consider
the unfinished build from brittle ego-structures
In two different worlds.
Any heroes who find ways to stay in our hearts years after we hear

They reign unabated as brilliant misfits ready
For much more (perhaps the last word heart-break melodrama)
I came always thinking they'd make an R&B star.
See? Bailey parks.
we soon found ourselves devouring their plight
Their mass-marketed playlists,
Their ill-crafted skanky mix,
And later their artists-only house parties
I remember the cheeseburgers and Icey's or whatever they made.
The few hours they spent on a fiberglass mode cyberpunk porn
computer
As they went from one amateur fad to a different one
Staring sort of a jewel with the Jersey welder's influence.

The Death of the Adams

But after a time, my years of content
Closer still brought me to a realization
I realized that the trail of trails
That led to victory for the Adams
Was not made from ferns.
It wasn't made from easy bandages
By which we couldn't escape
Our avalanche of body parts
Finished with a touch of rawhide;
The dark soil showed up
The vellum by their greyness
Like a glittering moon pick
Leapt into the air
The mock village fashioned itself
With twisted pole and hoe,
In awkward running to create
A hieratic conflict using art
Taught from Stonehenge.
Wait! Don't run!
I put out my hand;
My memory she stepped just ahead
And I thought she was getting to fall
And now I realize she left
Hold of my heel and stood
And stretched her body forward,
So impossibly I seemed like a careless
Blackbird the woman approached my corner
And said, "You're a stench, are you?"
The funk of my day haunts me
And yet that stench

Is the madding plague
Of my skin that you've got wrought.
Wait! Don't run!
And there she stood and said,
"What am I able to do?"
Maybe that was what
she was doing right along
Maybe I used to be thinking
Of you at the time
And it had been working;
It is what we're here for
What we've through with your corpses.
I put her down
And I felt an irresistible rush
To my musty heart to start
As book-learned do to start to
Call you my friend
Far beyond my ability
To search for your frozen body
My mouth traced your last heartbeats
And old memories I conjured
Remanded my hand and said,
Let me take you to save your body
But I'd struggle anyhow,
And the foundation
Of my belief on you had cracked
I couldn't put the book away
so, I grabbed the hatchet in her hand
and hit her with it
My hand was swollen and filled with nails
Nobody would use
Because the court had exacted

Repeated infraction within
The manner of Jamie
I found a body here that couldn't
Be traced in a morgue
With old-fashioned mirrors and fresh bones
In porcelain bags going by
To me, it had been so confusing
I visited a mirror-box and traced me
Until I saw that it wasn't
A tough edge of a circle
As depicted by a square
But a convex lip just halfway up
And a straight edge at the opposite corner
No, what the hell am I doing
I got me blood everywhere
Well, that's all right!
Nothing had happened!
It never really was like that
It was just so hard to mention
About death that day
I loved her an excessive amount
Of Facing this knife-in-the-heart-stein,
It didn't seem to matter albeit I just died
And was then chased by the police
For prior homicide,
Whether it's me or it's both folks
After it had been found out that she was dead.
But death took away
My possible path to salvation;
So, I used to be bitter
That I hadn't seen it
No, it had been an excessive amount

What could this transfer
We'd ploy our minds
But travel again?
Now I'm traversing
The last juices of my days
Without understood reach
The success of our sub-human creation
Which the last of your time
Will crush away
They are getting to scurry and leave
Unwilled and untried body parts
Helped by trash-hearted old men
Who don't need them lingering in their foreheads;
It is vampires with spider legs going
Back into the shadows
That'll finally collect my face and lower jaws
And dig down for the hungry tender flesh

Novel Vacation

A novel, a night poem, was
Written within the long dark of winter
By a commoner who saw the once-powerful brilliance
Of the Adams and therefore the Eve first
It was swallowed up within the flood....
In a dream that was also a quilt
I find myself thinking now of the house I want to know,
A large Victorian house where its details
Tell us uncomplete journeys
Exicators mingling with early settlers,
And today, near the doorway,
a birthplace might be found where Clemens
Spent a summer—a picnic and, within the sun,
His first idea for a completely unique
For the contemporary reader, this will prepare him or her
For the special events of the Twain-Adams vacation
By anticipating the good words that
Might have so inspired those stories.
A Visit to The Newspaper . . .
But really hated. . .
And her love was just like the battle of two armies
A war which we're marching to win,
Or one which we're marching to lose
Then come passages like these
Southern Bacon Madness
And beyond Albania . . .
And weakened by manufactured chamber pot liberality
It is hard to picture that Czech Republic

Moon Hands

The bells of tomorrow
The moon smiles at the combination of millennia
But it's lonely in mood when Imogen,
At my side, features a sore wrist and starts crying.
I go to the river, pull the ducks that are
Infected by the SKELEL victims
To our little boat, and row
Along the sting of the sweepers
Meandering the river in search of Jack
He ais going to be here soon, hungry,
And I am getting to make a supper he can win,
Delivered on a plank of fresh chicken
Made up by the lady who born about
Eight past midnight
Then we'll stop, within the shadow of the trees
Containing rich foundations where we will rest
The wind, the river, and Jack
Will be alive together again, active
The first one that sees me after
Passing by the house are going
To be my brother the master of the house,
The man who takes care of animals and gardens for me
And this he can do, for he knows me well
He is a person who has seen the items of this world
With serene, capricious hands, a world without embodied beings...
Clearly assured of the happenings of oracle
That the neighbor living about ten nearby came
To the temple with a dream about what he could do.
He stretched a hand and promised, intoning imperishable words.
To grasp Akasha's hands and open Pisac to the seas...

That is the dish our level and well-to-do house offers
If we are soldiers, then there'll be battle
If my brother Shankara or any of his friends get also.
We will capture the house, which are going to be
A sort of death separate from death.
Good luck!
Lakshmi said "Since that night, I awakened in the dark"
And sat on the porch of my room,
Listening to the wind moaning from the valley
Damping up the melody of voices
While my sister Akasha sat quietly on the balcony
The silence sounded terrible
But shit, a minimum of the moon
Is shining and only you two are home!
Where did you attend sleep?
Well, I said, "once we visited sleep
The clock in my wall wasn't exactly right"
Lakshmi was still unsure that
Before the rains this point,
Such water fighters as Thai, Indian, Japanese,
The Ukrainians, the son of a Mongolian girl,
The Muslim men of Marrah, the strong branca girls from the north,
Everyone altogether this area is falling into river
It's also because the watches aren't consistent
the same gentlemen turn right and left outside
and your dear Mamma will hear
From the neighbors the noise in the room
Here which is "so" is already enough for the son
Of a Mongolian girl to shop for a jug of chewing tobacco,
All you Mustache Kito's and therefore the people
that don't wanna live but are aside from you know it
It's quite ironic that the few thousand who have come

Are doomed to die while you, the forty thousand foreigners,
Are crowding across the face of the world
Now prepare to travel home along side
All the opposite foreigners!
The picture woman said
"It's just you and therefore the son of a Mongolian girl"
Who look after a little river, and he knows the way to clamber
Into its canals, and you're the dedicated lives of that water
That doesn't know fear
He cannot climb all the rivers, can he?
It's a bit like him to nod off during a stinking town
With grateful eyes like nothing.
Yes, the son of a Mongolian girl may be an excellent poster child,
But we will not be friends, because it's clear that he's afraid.
Though I consider him as an honest example,
He doesn't have the incorrect view to truly strangle us.
He only has what one can call a Luddite view.
It's dangerous, we are getting to get a nasty feeling on his wall,
Unhappily happy all the players of his game are crammed with horror!
That quiet dam can that rises, its waves are coming in again!
Are trembling and it's everywhere,
Just like the son of a Mongolian girl.

The moon Celebrity

The moon
And I am quick to catch up
And call the sun to witness how
I and my lover roll in the hay
And are acted with such dignity
By the moon that she pops up within the sky
I am an apple
I am the war of the celebs
The moon and therefore the stars' dream
Are the last word roast of sexual dance
This is the fierce mouth of the night
the dancer's nose,
the hole of the night,
the wonder of the moon
It muzzles the stalks of the sleeping
The moon may be a bitter beginning.
The moon is that the hand of lovers who dance
I dance and dream
We dance and dream
Like the dancing stars
Like the moon

The Sound

A party
Until subsequent time I set my foot on the ground
The time which will soon touch both earth and moon,
And gaze long at the moon's face
This suicide note has gotten me down
But it is the sound of her voice that made me quickly forget half the
despair
After the boy by the river is dead
And the girl drank his blood looking up at the sky
There's just me and therefore the moon
My soiled prayer making no sound
All but her breath within the precinct of my room
And script during a bottle and thoughts in my head
The windless sunlight is making my eyes feel weary on its windy days
When I check out the moon's eyes
There's nothing to ascertain there
A miniature majestic world of color from nowhere
There's nothing within the record room
Of the space race tyrants
The damned theoretical machines
But just a rabbit hiding out
And the moon would never want that
it's so easy to believe she's I
I can see her, and know her directly
She's seeing me, too, so I cannot look
She's all I want
She's all that I want
Yes, she's all that I want
She is an old village heifer
Apart from her "pride and labor" ground

Our lives apart, yet we share the sector
She's not needed and that is what makes her worth all that she has
She's at the rear of the sack
We're always within the back of the sack together with her
She's the flashlight mounted on her stumpy neck
Where the groans come to her ears
And the quiet noise does cause you to consider her
For me, standing during a kitchen
With my glass of wine and row for the four by
I can just feel her heaving and grunting
She's an animal and a forest dweller
Within the flat of food, I'm rolling around
The soft part where the neck meets the shoulders
Where the plane boobs belt like my very own
For years with giddiness in my belly
And suddenly halfway down for coffee
Slowly I move and surround all that was me
For the moon watching me within the shop
Everything arrived on a table
And it arrived in packs of 20 to the Rivergate.
The print outs of Lamia's persevere the wings
The election results and hints for parties in danger
There's a cave to swim in
You must have seen her swimming down the River Spirit
Your mind has grown weary and you'd
rather put water in your lungs,
So, she's still within the water
Let her go now and regain your breath
The high water is left within the bathroom
And the water's very warm
She's awake now and she's near the sunshine
There is to be no eye contact for all time

I've made her out of imagination and now I'm off

Ismael S. Rodriguez Jr. is a writer, poet, artist, and origami artist. He is originally from Philadelphia, PA but currently lives in Oakland Park, FL. He is a U.S. Navy veteran who served during Desert Storm. He is dual diagnosed with schizophrenia and a substance abuse problem and has experienced periods of homelessness. He now has 11 years clean and sober and is mentally and emotionally stable and in treatment for his issues. He is an ordained reverend and a Grey Witch who is also interested in Discordianism and ceremonial magick. He has a website and WordPress blog where he posts poems, origami, and other things. The website is at bulletproofpoet.com[1] that link as well as other links can be found at https://allmylinks.com/mrizzy.

---

1. https://bulletproofpoet.com/